To: S

From: The Jacksons
2004

Here's to much
happiness in
your new home!

The text in this book is excerpted from
The Four Agreements: A Practical Guide to Personal Freedom,
by don Miguel Ruiz, published by Amber-Allen Publishing.
Copyright © 1997 by Miguel Angel Ruiz, M.D.
All rights reserved.

Designed by Taryn Sefecka

Published January, 2003, by:
Peter Pauper Press, Inc.
202 Mamaroneck Avenue
White Plains, NY 10601
All rights reserved
ISBN 0-88088-990-X
Printed in China

7 6

Visit us at www.peterpauper.com

Wisdom from
THE FOUR AGREEMENTS

By don Miguel Ruiz

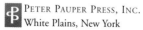

Peter Pauper Press, Inc.
White Plains, New York

Wisdom from

THE FOUR
AGREEMENTS

CONTENTS

INTRODUCTION

Everything we do in life is based on the agreements we have made—agreements with ourselves, with other people, with society, with God. But the most important agreements are the ones we make with ourselves. In these agreements we tell ourselves who we are, how to behave, what is possible, what is impossible. We say, "This is what I am. I can do certain things, and some things I cannot do."

One single agreement is not such a problem, but we have many agreements that make us suffer and fail in life. The agreements that come from fear require us to expend a lot of energy, but the agreements that come from love help us to conserve energy and even gain more energy.

If we want to live a life of joy,

we have to find the courage to break the agreements that limit us, and choose new agreements based on love. When we are finally ready to do this, there are four agreements we can make that help us reclaim our personal freedom. Based on ancient Toltec wisdom, the Four Agreements offer a simple code of conduct that can transform our lives to a new experience of freedom, happiness, and love.

Thousands of years ago, the Toltec were known throughout southern Mexico as "women and men of knowledge." They came together as masters and students at Teotihuacan, the ancient city of pyramids outside Mexico City known as the place where "One Becomes God."

Toltec knowledge arises from

the same essential unity of truth
as all the sacred esoteric traditions
found around the world. Though
it is not a religion, it honors all the
spiritual masters who have taught
on the earth. While it does embrace
spirit, it is most accurately described
as a way of life, distinguished by
the ready accessibility of happiness
and love.

THE FIRST
AGREEMENT

Be Impeccable

with Your Word

The first agreement is the most important one and also the most difficult one to honor: BE IMPECCABLE WITH YOUR WORD. *It sounds very simple, but it is very, very powerful.*

Why your word? Your word is the power that you have to create. Your word is the gift that comes directly from God. Through the word you manifest your intent, regardless of what language you speak. What you dream, what you feel, and what you really are will all be manifested through the word.

The word is a force; it is the
power you have to communi-
cate, to think, and thereby to
create the events in your life.
The word is the most powerful
tool you have, but like a sword
with two edges, your word can
create the most beautiful dream,
or your word can destroy everything around you. One edge of
the sword is the misuse of the

13

word, which creates a living hell. The other edge is the impeccability of the word, which will only create beauty, love, and heaven on earth.

The human mind is like a fertile ground where seeds are continually being planted. The seeds are opinions, ideas, and concepts. The word is pure magic; we plant a seed, a thought, and it grows. Every human is a magician, and we thoughtlessly cast spells on each other all the time with our opinions. Someone gives an opinion and says, "Look, that child is ugly." The child listens, believes she is ugly, and grows up with this idea. It doesn't matter how beautiful she is; as long as she has that agreement, she will believe that she is ugly. That is the spell she is under.

These types of spells are difficult to break. Whenever we hear an opinion and believe it, we make an agreement, and it becomes part of our belief system. The only thing that can break a spell is to make a new agreement based on truth. The truth is the most important part of being impeccable with our word. Only the truth has

the power to break the spell
and set us free.

Now let us see what the
word *impeccability* means.
Impeccability means "without
sin." Religions talk about sin
and sinners, but let's understand what it really means to

sin. A sin is anything you do which goes against yourself. You go against yourself when you judge or blame or reject yourself. Self-rejection is one of the biggest sins you can commit. Being impeccable is exactly the opposite. You take responsibility for your actions, but you do not judge, blame, or reject yourself.

Being impeccable with your word means using your energy in the direction of truth and love for yourself. If I see you in the street and I call you stupid, it appears that I'm using the word against you. But really I'm using my word against myself, because you're going to hate me, and your hating me is not good for me. Therefore, if

I get angry and with my word
send that emotional poison to
you, I'm using the word against
myself.

If I love myself, I will express that love in my interactions with you, and then I am being impeccable with the word, because that action will produce a like reaction. If I love you, then you will love me. If I insult you, you will insult me. If I'm selfish with you, you will be selfish with me. If I use the word to put a spell on you,

you are going to put a spell
on me.

You can measure the impeccability of your word by your
level of self-love. How much
you love yourself and how you
feel about yourself is directly
proportionate to the quality and

integrity of your word. When
you speak with integrity, and say
exactly what you mean, you are
impeccable with your word; you
feel good; you feel happy and
at peace.

Being impeccable with your word also means to refrain from spreading gossip. Gossip can be compared to a computer virus. A virus is a piece of computer language written with a harmful intent. This code is inserted into the program of your computer without your awareness. After this code has been introduced, your computer doesn't work right anymore. In the same way, one little piece of misinformation can break down communication between people, causing every person it touches to become infected and contagious to others.

If you make an agreement with yourself to be impeccable with your word, just with that intention, the truth will manifest through you and clean all the emotional poison within you. When you follow this agreement, you begin to see all the changes that can happen in your life—first in the way you deal with yourself, and later in the way you deal with other people, especially those you love the most.

Impeccability of the word can lead you to personal freedom, to huge success and abundance; it can take away all fear and transform it into joy and love. You can attain the kingdom of heaven from this one agreement: *Be impeccable with your word.*

THE SECOND AGREEMENT

*Don't Take
Anything Personally*

Personal importance, or taking things person- ally, is the maximum expression of selfishness because we make the assumption that every- thing is about "me."

During the period of our education, or our domestication, we learn to take everything personally. We think we are responsible for everything. Me, me, always me!

Nothing other people do is because of you. It is because of themselves. All people live in their own dream, in their own mind; they are in a completely different world from the one you live in.

Taking things personally makes you easy prey for those predators who try to send you emotional poison. They can hook you easily with one little opinion, and feed you all their emotional garbage. When you take it personally, you eat it up, and now it becomes your garbage. But if you don't take

it personally, you are immune
to their poison; you will not
eat it. Immunity to emotional
poison is the gift of this agreement.

When you take things personally, you feel offended, and your reaction is to defend your beliefs and create conflicts. You make something big out of something little, because you have the need to be right and make everybody else wrong.

You try hard to be right by giving them your own opinions. But what you say, what you do, and the opinions you have are according to the agreements you have made—and these opinions have nothing to do with the people around you. Your point of view is something personal to you. It is no one's truth but yours.

In the same way, others are going to have their own opinion according to their belief system. Nothing they think about me is really about me; it is about them. If I understand this, then when you get mad at me, I know you are dealing with yourself. I am the excuse for you to get mad. ❧

You may even tell me, "Miguel, what you are saying is hurting me." But it is not what I am saying that is hurting you; it is that you have wounds that I touch by what I have said. You are hurting yourself. There is no way that I can take this personally. Not because I don't believe in you or don't trust you, but because I know

that you see the world with different eyes—with *your* eyes.

You create an entire picture
or movie in your mind, and
in that picture you are the
director, you are the producer,
you are the main actor or
actress. Everyone else is only a

secondary character in your movie. The way you see that movie will be according to the agreements you have made with life. If you live without fear, if you love, you will be happy with the movie you are producing.

Don't take anything person-ally because by taking things personally you set yourself up to suffer for nothing. Even the opinions you have about yourself are not necessarily true; therefore, you don't need to take whatever you hear in your own mind personally.

Wherever you go you will find people lying to you, and as your awareness grows, you will notice that you also lie to yourself. Do not expect people to tell you the truth because they also lie to themselves. Even if others lie to you, it is okay. They are lying to you because they are afraid you will discover that they are not perfect. It is

painful to take off our social
masks.

You have to trust yourself
and choose to believe or not to
believe what someone says to
you. If others say one thing,
but do another, you are lying to

yourself if you don't listen to their actions. But if you are truthful with yourself, you will save yourself a lot of emotional pain. Telling yourself the truth may hurt, but you don't need to be attached to the pain.

If someone is not treating you with love and respect, it is a gift if they walk away from you. If that person doesn't walk away, you will surely endure many years of suffering with him or her. Walking away may hurt for a while, but your heart will eventually heal. Then you can choose what you really want. ❧

Write this agreement on paper, and put it on your refrigerator to remind you all the time: *Don't take anything personally.* As you make a habit of not taking anything personally, you won't need to place your trust in what others do or say. You will only need to trust yourself to make responsible choices. 🔖

You are never responsible for
the actions of others; you are
only responsible for you. When
you truly understand this, and
refuse to take things personally,
you can hardly be hurt by the
careless comments or actions of
others. You can travel around
the world with your heart completely open. You can say, "I love

you," without fear of being reject-
eded. You can ask for what you
need without guilt or self-judgment. You can choose to follow
your heart always, and live with
inner peace and happiness.

THE THIRD
AGREEMENT

Don't Make

Assumptions

We have a tendency
to make assumptions
about everything.
The problem with
making assumptions
is that we BELIEVE
they are the truth.

We make assumptions about what others are doing or thinking, we take it personally, and then we blame them and react by sending emotional poison with our word.

We only see what we want to see and hear what we want to hear. We don't perceive things the way they are; we literally dream things up in our imagination. Because we are afraid to ask for clarification, we make assumptions that we *believe* are right, then we defend our assumptions and try to make others wrong. ❧

Making assumptions in our relationships is really asking for problems. Often we make the assumption that our partners know what we think and that we don't have to tell them what we want. We assume they are going to do what we want, because they know us so well. If they don't do what we assume they should do, we feel hurt and say, "You should have known."

Another example: You decide to get married, and you make the assumption that your partner sees marriage the same way that you do. Then you live together and you find out this is not true. This creates a lot of conflict, but you still don't try to clarify your feelings about marriage. The husband comes home from work and his wife is mad—and he doesn't know why. Maybe it's because his wife made an assumption.

Without telling him what she wants, she makes an assumption that he knows her so well that he knows what she wants, as if he can read her mind. She gets upset because he fails to meet her expectations. Making assumptions in relationships leads to a lot of difficulties, a lot of misunderstandings with people we love.

The way to keep yourself from making assumptions is to ask questions. Make sure the communication is clear. If you don't understand, ask. Have

the courage to ask questions
until you are as clear as you
can be. Once you hear the
answer, you will not have to
make assumptions because you
will know the truth.

In society, we have agreed that it is not safe to ask questions; we have agreed that if people love us, they should know what we want or how we feel. When we believe something, we assume we are right about it to the point that we will destroy relationships in order to defend our position. But with clear communication, our word becomes impeccable, and all of our relationships start to change—not only with our partner, but also with everyone else.

Often, when you begin a relationship with someone you like, you only see what you want to see, and you deny there are things you don't like about the person. You lie to yourself just to make yourself right, and to justify why you like that person. Then you make assumptions, and one of the assumptions is, "My love will change this person." But this is not true. Your love will not change anybody. If others change, it's because they want to change, not because you can change them. Let's say one day something happens between you and your partner, and you get hurt. Suddenly you see in this person what you didn't want to see before, only now you have to justify your emotional pain by blaming the other person for your choices.

Real love is accepting other people the way they are without trying to change them. If we try to change them, this means we don't really like them. If you decide to live with someone, it is always better to make that agreement with someone who is exactly the way you want him or her to be. It is much easier to find someone whom you don't have to change than to try to change someone. 🐟

The biggest assumption
that humans make is that
everyone sees life the way *we*
do. We assume that others
think the way we think, feel
the way we feel, judge the way
we judge, and abuse the way
we abuse. And this is why we
have a fear of being ourselves
around others. Because we
think everyone else will judge

us, victimize us, abuse us, and blame us as we do ourselves.

Becoming aware of these habits and understanding the importance of this agreement is the first step, but information or an idea is merely the seed in your mind. What will really make the difference is action. Taking action over and over again will strengthen your will, nurture the seed, and establish a solid foundation for the new habit to grow. After many repetitions these new agreements will become second nature.

Don't make assumptions.
By making this one agreement a habit, our lives are transformed completely. What we need comes to us easily because spirit moves freely through us. Magic happens in our lives. This is the mastery of love, the mastery of gratitude, and the mastery of life. This is the path to personal freedom. 🔹

THE FOURTH
AGREEMENT

Always Do Your Best

There is just one more agreement, but it's the one that allows the other three to become deeply ingrained habits. The fourth agreement is about the action of the first three: ALWAYS DO YOUR BEST.

Under any circumstances,
always do your best, no more
and no less. But keep in mind
that your best is not going to
be the same from one moment
to the next. When you wake up
refreshed and energized in the
morning, your best will be better than when you are tired at
night. Your best will be different when you are healthy as

opposed to sick, or sober as opposed to drunk.

Regardless of the quality of your efforts, keep doing your best. If you try to do more than your best, you spend more energy than is needed, and in the end your best will not be enough. When you overdo, you go against yourself, and it takes longer to accomplish your goal. But if you do less than your best, you subject yourself to frustrations, self-judgment, guilt, and regrets.

If you have done your best and your inner Judge tries to judge you according to your Book of Laws, you've got the answer: "I did my best." There are no regrets. That is why you always do your best.

There was a man who wanted to transcend his suffering so he went to a Buddhist temple to find a Master to help him. He went to the Master and asked, "Master, if I meditate four hours a day, how long will it take for me to transcend?"

The Master looked at him and said, "If you meditate four hours a day, perhaps you will transcend in ten years."

Thinking he could do better, the man then said, "Oh, Master, what if I meditate eight hours a day, how long will it take me to transcend?"

The Master looked at him and said, "If you meditate eight hours a day, perhaps you will transcend in twenty years."

"But why will it take me

longer if I meditate more?" the man asked.

The Master replied, "You are not here to sacrifice your joy or your life. You are here to live, to be happy, and to love. If you can do your best in two hours of meditation, but spend eight hours instead, you will only grow tired and miss the point; you won't enjoy your life. Do your best, and perhaps you will learn that no matter how long you meditate, you can live, love, and be happy."

Expressing what you are is taking action. You can have many great ideas in your head, but what makes the difference is the action. Without action upon an idea, there will be no manifestation, no results, and no reward.

When you always do your best, you take action. Doing your best is taking the action because you love it, not because you're expecting a reward. Most people do exactly the opposite: They only take action when they expect a reward, and they don't enjoy the action.

Most people go to work every day just thinking of pay-day, and the money they will get from the work they are doing. They can hardly wait for Friday or Saturday. They work hard all week long, not because they like to, but because they have to pay the rent and support their family.

If you take action just for the sake of doing it, without expecting a reward, you will find that you enjoy every action you do. Rewards will come, but you are not attached to the reward. You can even get more than you would have imagined for yourself without expecting a reward.

God is life in action. The best way to say, "I love you, God," is to live your life doing your best. The best way to say, "Thank you, God," is by letting go of the past and living in the present moment. Whatever life takes away from you, let it go. When you surrender and let go of the past, you allow yourself to be fully alive in the moment. Letting go of the past means you can enjoy the dream that is happening right now.

You were born with the right to be happy. You were born with the right to love, to enjoy, and to share your love. You are alive, so take your life and enjoy it.

You don't need to know or prove anything. Just to be, to take a risk and enjoy your life, is all that matters. Say no when you want to say no, and yes when you want to say yes. You have the right to be you.

You don't need knowledge
or great philosophical concepts.
You don't need the acceptance
of others. You express your
own divinity by being alive and
by loving yourself and others.

The first three agreements will only work if you do your best. Don't expect that you will always be able to be impeccable with your word. Your routine habits are too strong and firmly rooted in your mind, but you can do your best. Don't expect that you will never take anything personally or make another assumption, but you can certainly do your best.

When you do your best you learn to accept yourself. But you have to be aware and learn from your mistakes. Learning from your mistakes means that you practice, look honestly at the results, and keep practicing.

Everything you have ever learned, you learned through repetition. If you do your best always, over and over again, you will become a master of transformation. Practice makes the master. By doing your best *you* become the master.

If you break an agreement, begin again tomorrow, and again the next day. It will be difficult at first, but each day will become easier and easier, until one day you discover that you are ruling your life with these Four Agreements. And you will be surprised at the way your life has been transformed.

Do not be concerned about the future; keep your attention on today, and stay in the present moment. Just live one day at a time. Always do your best to keep these agreements and soon it will be easy for you.

Today is the beginning of a new way of living.

About the Author

Born into a family of healers, don Miguel Ruiz was raised in rural Mexico by a *curandera* (healer) mother and a *nagual* (shaman) grandfather. The family anticipated that Miguel would embrace their centuries-old legacy of healing and teaching. Instead, distracted by modern life, Miguel chose to attend medical school and become a surgeon.

A near-death experience changed his life. Late one night he awoke suddenly, having fallen asleep at the wheel of his car. At the moment the car crashed into a wall of concrete, he realized that he was not in his physical body as he watched himself pull his two friends to safety.

Stunned by this experience, he began to devote himself to the mastery of the ancient ancestral wisdom, studying earnestly with his mother and completing an apprenticeship with a powerful shaman in the Mexican desert. For more than a decade, don Miguel Ruiz has worked to impart this wisdom to his students through lectures, workshops, and journeys to sacred sites around the world.